THE ADVENTURES OF BUTT BOY & TIGGER

a play by Steven Dawson

THE ADVENTURES OF BUTT BOY & TIGGER
a play by Steven Dawson

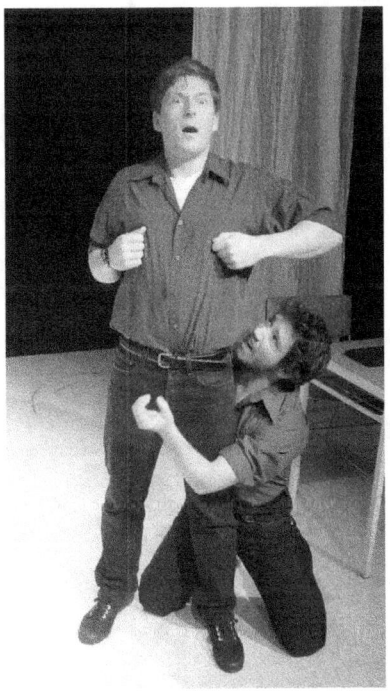

Angus Brown & Felix Allsop at the Edinburgh Fringe 2008.

First Printing: 2015

ISBN 978-1-326-17327-2

Out Cast Theatre
PO Box 77
Craigieburn, VIC, AUSTRALIA 3064

www.outcast.org.au

Any application for performance must be made to:

RICK RAFTOS MANAGEMENT PTY LTD
P.O. Box 445, Paddington
NSW, Australia, 2021
Telephone 61 2 9281 9622
Fax 61 2 92127100
raftos@raftos.com.au

Cover Photo by James Penlidis.

Front Cover: *Felix Allsop & Angus Brown from the 2008 Edinburgh production.*

THE ADVENTURES OF BUTT BOY & TIGGER
a play by Steven Dawson

Characters

MATT
JAMIE

An earlier version of this play was first performed July 4th, 2007
Mechanics Institute Performing Arts Centre, Melbourne

Cast

JAMIE   Alex Christopolous
MATT   Felix Allsop

Alex Christopolous & Felix Allsop

This version was first performed July 2008
Mechanics Institute Performing Arts Centre, Melbourne

JAMIE   Angus Brown
MATT   Felix Allsop

Directed by Steven Dawson
Produced by Adrian Corbett & Out Cast Theatre

THE ADVENTURES OF BUTT BOY & TIGGER
a play by Steven Dawson

SCENE ONE

LATE NIGHT. JAMIE SITS AT HIS COMPUTER. HE PAUSES FOR A MOMENT THEN HITS A KEY. THERE IS AN AUDIBLE DING ON THE OTHER COMPUTER. MATT POPS HIS HEAD OUT OF THE WINGS. HE MOVES TOWARDS HIS COMPUTER.

MATT
That'd be right. Two hours of diddly-squat and just as I'm about to go to bed...

HE LOOKS AT THE MONITOR

Hello. Who are we then?

HE LOOKS A LITTLE CLOSER.

Bloody hell. Sorry weirdo. Not interested.

HE STARTS TO WALK AWAY THEN STOPS.

Maybe just a quick peek.

HE GOES BACK TO THE COMPUTER. HE TYPES.

Hi.

JAMIE TYPES BACK

JAMIE
Hi.

MATT
Bit late.

JAMIE
I know. Couldn't sleep.

MATT
That's okay.

JAMIE
You want to talk?

MATT
What did you have in mind?

JAMIE
Nothing really.

MATT
Well it's bloody freezing and I have a very fluffy doona with my name on it so you better have something to keep me from it.

JAMIE
Sorry. If you want to go...

MATT
No, that's cool.

JAMIE
Are you alone?

MATT
It's kinda hard for more than one person to type on the same keyboard so yeah, I am alone.

JAMIE
Okay.

MATT
Interesting handle.

JAMIE
Is it?

MATT
You don't think so? You don't think *Butt Boy* is an interesting name? Not exactly subtle, is it?

JAMIE
It wasn't my first choice.

MATT
Really?

JAMIE
No. I'm a bit of a comic geek. I was trying to do Batman but that was taken. So I tried Bat Boy but I was so tired I made a typo. Then I started getting all these replies so I thought…what the hell.

MATT
I'm not surprised. Pretty much spells it out, don't you think? You know, you might want to think about changing your profile name.

JAMIE
Maybe.

MATT
Bet it attracts a lot of loonies.

JAMIE
A few. You're the first one I tried to contact, though.

MATT
Well, I feel special. What singled me out?

JAMIE
From your profile you seem nice.

MATT
Well, that's what they said on my last parole report. *[BEAT]* I'm joking. I must say you don't give much away on yours, do you? *[READS ALOUD]* "Clean cut. Love movies and talking" That's a lot of detail. One step short of Amish.

JAMIE
I like your name.

MATT
My name?

JAMIE
On your profile. Sounds nice as well.

MATT
Uh-huh.

JAMIE
So why do you call yourself Tigger? Unless that's your real name?

MATT
What?

JAMIE
Sounds kind of Middle Eastern. Is it?

MATT
It's from Winnie The Pooh.

JAMIE
Winnie the Pooh?

MATT
The book. You know. Tiggers can bounce. *[PAUSE]* I thought it was cute. Maybe I was wrong.

JAMIE
I like your picture.

MATT
Thank you. I like your picture too.

JAMIE
Yeah? A friend took it a few years back.

MATT
"Friend" friend or euphemism friend?

JAMIE
What's that?

MATT
What's what?

JAMIE
What you said. *[TYPING IT OUT]* Euphemism.

MATT
Oh, um…was he a real friend or a boyfriend?

JAMIE
She was a girl. I mean, she is a girl. I don't have a boyfriend. You?

MATT
None I'll admit to. It's a nice photo.

JAMIE
Yeah, I thought so too.

MATT
She must *really* like you.

JAMIE
She did.

MATT
You're speaking in the past tense.

JAMIE
She stopped talking to me five years ago when I told her I was…you know.

MATT
So that photo's at least 5 years old?

JAMIE
I still look pretty much the same.

MATT
Yeah. They all say that. Or they've Photo-shopped themselves into a blur.

JAMIE
Do they? You do this a lot then?

MATT
Do what?

JAMIE
Chat people up online.

MATT
Chat *to*. Not chat up. There's a difference. And don't forget, you dinged me. So how long have you known you were…"you know"?

JAMIE
6 years.

MATT
So you should be good at it by now. Right?

JAMIE
I guess.

MATT
Enough to not call it "you know"?

JAMIE
I guess.

MATT
Sorry. I'm getting heavy.

JAMIE
That's okay.

MATT
That's not what this is all about.

JAMIE
What's what all about?

MATT
This. What we're doing.

JAMIE
We're not doing anything.

MATT
Not yet. So…

JAMIE
So?

MATT
So…you wanna play?

JAMIE
Play?

MATT
That's right.

JAMIE
Play what?

MATT
I don't know. Fucking Monopoly. Play! *[PAUSE]* It means have sex.

JAMIE
Then why didn't you just say that?

MATT
I was trying to be subtle.

JAMIE
Subtle? Your profile says you have an eight inch dick. In bold! I think that ship has sailed. *[BEAT]* What did you have in mind anyway?

MATT
What I have in mind should be a surprise, don't you think? I don't want to give away the game plan too soon. Do you want to meet up? Where do you live?

JAMIE
Frankston.

MATT
Shit.

JAMIE
You?

MATT
Sunbury.

JAMIE
Is that too far?

MATT
May as well be on another planet.

JAMIE
I could drive to your place...

MATT
Great!

JAMIE
...if my car wasn't getting fixed.

MATT
Great.

JAMIE
We don't have to meet tonight. We could meet later.

MATT
I guess.

JAMIE
I can't really have you over at my place anyway at the moment.

MATT
Place a pig sty?

JAMIE
No. Mum keeps it pretty clean.

MATT
You live with your mum?!!

JAMIE
Yeah.

MATT
Jesus! How old are you?

JAMIE
Twenty four. You?

MATT
Same *[PAUSE]* -ish.

JAMIE
That was vague.

MATT
Would you like to see my carbon dating?

JAMIE
You meet many people doing this?

MATT
Guys! Do I meet many guys?!

JAMIE
I guess that's what I meant.

MATT
This is the first time.

JAMIE
Really?

MATT
Of course not! Do I sound like a virgin?

JAMIE
No. *[PAUSE]* Do I?

MATT
Yes. As a matter of fact you do.

JAMIE
Oh.

MATT
[PAUSE] Oh shit. You *are* a virgin, aren't you?

JAMIE
No, I'm...

MATT
You are! I'll bet you're just some spotty little 14 year old getting your jollies whacking off some knuckle-children on Mum's broadband account while she's passed out behind the telly. Tell me!

JAMIE
I'm not.

MATT
Which part?

JAMIE
I'm not a virgin.

MATT
How many men have you had sex with? And I don't mean quick groin grabs at scout camp with all those other greasy netball jocks, but real hands-on suck'n'fuck fests with real men.

JAMIE SAYS NOTHING

Hellooo?

JAMIE
I was just thinking.

MATT
It wasn't a trick question.

JAMIE
Three.

MATT
Three?

JAMIE
Yeah.

MATT
You're cruising Gaydar profiles already and you've only had sex 3 times?

JAMIE
I've had sex lots of times. Just with three men.

MATT
Please tell me it was all at the same time because that's gonna win you big brownie points.

JAMIE
No. They were all separate and that was a while ago.

MATT
Define a while ago. More than a year?

JAMIE
I guess.

MATT
And where did you meet them? Online?

JAMIE
No. I've only been on line twice.

MATT
Bars, clubs, beats?

JAMIE
Friends of friends.

MATT
Wish I had me some friends like that. Could do with the outsourcing. So I take it you're not a scene queen?

JAMIE
No.

MATT
And you don't go to the clubs?

JAMIE
No.

MATT
Dance parties?

JAMIE
Hate loud music.

MATT
Saunas?

JAMIE
Allergic to ammonia.

MATT
How about show tunes?

JAMIE
You want me to sing one?

MATT
No, do you like them?

JAMIE
I saw Annie 3 times. Does that make me a show queen?

MATT
No. Just retarded.

JAMIE
Great. I just like music. Good female singers. Joni Mitchell, Janis Ian.

MATT
Bloody hell. No wonder you've only had sex with 3 guys.

JAMIE
Are you a show queen?

MATT
Fuck no. I've got about 5 years before that happens. My last boyfriend was, though. Part of the flight plan for most gay guys over 30, I think. Show queen, rice queen, old queen, dead queen.

JAMIE
Something to look forward to.

MATT
You betcha.

JAMIE
You had many boyfriends?

MATT
Plenty.

JAMIE
What happened to them?

MATT
They all met each other at my last birthday and decided they hated me. Now they all go out each month for dinner and email me the pictures. Bastards. Speaking of which...you got any other pictures of yourself?

JAMIE
My scanner's broken.

MATT
How convenient. Describe yourself then.

JAMIE
Um. I'm...I'm 5 foot 7.

MATT
Good.

JAMIE
Slim. Clean shaven.

MATT
I can see that on your photo. Even though it's five years old. And your nether regions? Give me a little info to go by. I need to put the picture together a bit more.

JAMIE
Oh. Um....14.

MATT
Bloody hell! *[PAUSE]* Oh, wait a minute. You're talking metric, aren't you?

JAMIE
Yeah.

MATT
Thank God. My head was spinning. When it comes to dick size never talk metric It's liable to bring on a stroke.

JAMIE
And what about you?

MATT
I've put everything worth mentioning on my profile.

JAMIE
Okay.

MATT
So, it's late. You still want to play?

JAMIE
I thought we weren't going to meet. Might be hard trying to meet up now.

MATT
We can still have fun just talking.

JAMIE
Can we?

MATT
Sure. We can do plenty. How good a typist are you?

JAMIE
Pretty fast.

MATT
That's gonna help. What kind of fantasies do you have?

JAMIE
I haven't really thought about it.

MATT
Well, try. Are you into sport?

JAMIE
Sometimes.

MATT
That's good. I like footy.

JAMIE
I don't know anything about footy.

MATT
How about soccer?

JAMIE
Even less.

MATT
That's cool. Just fake it. *[HE STARTS TYPING]* Okay. So it's after the semi-final. All the other team members have gone for the day, the crowds have left. Just the rookie alone in the locker room. That's you.

JAMIE GETS UP AND STARTS ACTING OUT THE SCENE

You start taking your gear off. Shoes and socks. Then you take off your shirt reveal-ing a well-chiseled chest. You sit on the bench in just your white shorts. Your legs spread apart slightly. You rub your upper thigh. It's still tender and slightly bruised already from the big dark dude on the other team taking you down in the first half.

JAMIE
What did he look like?

MATT
Big beautiful Maori fucker. You thought to yourself he was probably hung like a horse.

JAMIE
Is he?

MATT
Yeah probably but this story's not about him?

JAMIE
No?

MATT
No, now shut up.

JAMIE
Okay.

MATT
Where was I?

JAMIE
I was rubbing my bruise.

MATT
Ooh yeah. Rubbing your bruise. *[BEAT]* Right, rubbing your bruise. It still smarts a little but you reckon a nice hot shower is just the thing to fix it and you won't have any of the other players in the showers to distract you with their big dicks

JAMIE
Everyone has a big dick?

MATT
People don't have fantasies about small dicks. That'd be weird.

JAMIE
I get it.

MATT
But they're all ugly.

JAMIE
Pity.

MATT
Ssh! You're still on the bench. Your hand starts to move up your thigh.

JAMIE
Okay.

THEY MOVE INTO THE PLAYING AREA.

MATT
The air is a little moist from the shower. You carry on.

JAMIE
What? Oh, yeah. I stand up. I stand in front of the mirror. I wipe it down so I can see my shorts. I turn slightly and start to pull my shorts down a little. I reveal the tan line from my weekend at the beach. It stands out against my nice white arse.

MATT
It's a beautiful nice round arse. Like a peach.

JAMIE
Er, yeah. I start to pull my shorts down further.

MATT
All the while you're rubbing your crotch. It's starting to get hard.

JAMIE
I'm thinking…should I have a wank? No-one's around.

MATT
You should. You should.

JAMIE
I mean, I'm all alone.

MATT
So you think. *[HE GETS UP]* You haven't noticed the big burly coach coming into the change rooms. He's forty but he has a great body under that uniform. Looks like Tom Selleck. He stands near the door.

JAMIE
I always thought he was looking at me different to the other players.

MATT
He's standing at the doorway watching your hand rub up and down your crotch then follows your hand as it feels under the waist band and lets the shorts drop to the floor. I stand there with my big fat cock standing straight up.

JAMIE
A pigeon could perch on it.

MATT
What? Forget the pigeon!

JAMIE
Forgotten. My fat cock is pointing straight ahead.

MATT
How big is it?

JAMIE
It's pretty big.

MATT
Tell me!

JAMIE
I just told you. It's pretty big!

MATT
More info.

JAMIE
Massive. Long and thick. 10 inches. Like a tin can.

MATT
V size or Coke?

JAMIE
Coke.

MATT
Ooh.

JAMIE
Strong and fat enough to hold up a beach towel all by itself.

MATT
That's big.

JAMIE
Fucking huge!

MATT
Cut or uncut?

JAMIE
Cut. No. Uncut.

MATT
Make up your mind.

JAMIE
Um…uncut!

MATT
Ooh baby. And what's the coach doing? What am I doing?

JAMIE
You're still watching me.

MATT
I got that.

JAMIE
Your dick is starting to get hard.

MATT
It sure is.

JAMIE
Starting to make a bulge in your grey tracksuit pants.

MATT
I love grey track suit pants. You can see fucking everything! And I especially love the word 'bulge.' It's right up there with girth.

JAMIE
You've got no undies on so you've been swinging commando all afternoon during training and your balls are really hanging low.

MATT
How low?

JAMIE
Four inches down.

MATT
Bet they're sweaty and salty.

JAMIE
We don't know that yet, do we?

MATT
No.

JAMIE
Suddenly I feel your presence in the locker room.

MATT
I shove my hand inside my tracksuit pants so you don't see my massive hard on.

JAMIE
Another huge dick, huh?

MATT
Yeah!

JAMIE
Yeah. I look in the edge of the mirror and just see the edge of your tracksuit top. I realise it's you. But I don't want to say anything. Not yet. I want to see what would happen. I drop down and pull up my shorts real slow.

MATT
Giving me the full fruit basket.

JAMIE
I look around slowly. *[HE PUTS HIS LEG UP ON THE CHAIR]* "Hey coach."

MATT
"Hey Tommy." That's your name. "What you doing?"

JAMIE
Nothing Coach. Just pulled a hammy early on and wanted to see it didn't do any damage.

MATT
And did it?

JAMIE
Seems to be alright, coach. But you never know how these things can…*flare up.*

MATT
Tell me about it. Maybe I should take a quick look at it.

JAMIE
Don't you need to get home to your wife coach?

MATT
Oh, she uh…she died 3 days ago.

JAMIE
Really?

MATT
Yeah. Buried her yesterday. Tough break. Of course the kids will miss her but life goes on.

JAMIE
Where are they?

MATT
Oh, somewhere. So…let's have a look at that groin of yours.

HE DROPS DOWN IN FRONT OF JAMIE

JAMIE
It's my thigh actually.

MATT
[JUMPING UP] So you're a doctor as well? I'll be the judge of that.

JAMIE
I'm sure you know better, coach.

MATT
[DROPPING DOWN AGAIN AND PUTTING A HAND ON HIS THIGH] Now, where does it hurt exactly?

JAMIE
[MOVING MATT'S HAND CLOSER TO HIS CROTCH] Just there is a bit tender.

MATT
[STARTS RUBBING IT] Just here?

JAMIE
Uh-huh. Ooh that feels good.

MATT
I'll bet it does. I'll bet it does. You know what I think you need?

JAMIE
What's that, coach?

MATT
A bit of *deep tissue* massage.

JAMIE
Really?

MATT
The deeper the better.

JAMIE
I think you may be right.

MATT
But you really should get some heat on it first. Boy, that's some piece of meat you got on you kid.

JAMIE
You think so, coach?

MATT
Fine bit of meat like that should have plenty of admirers. I bet the girls really go for you.

JAMIE
They do coach but most can't handle the "girth."

MATT
[SHUDDERING] Oh dear god.

JAMIE
Yeah. They really have trouble with it. It's got a lot of girth.

MATT
Bloody hell.

JAMIE
"What a lot of girth" they say. *[COCKNEY ACCENT]* "It's a big bulge and no mistake."

MATT
What? You're doing accents now? We're typing this. I can't hear accents when you're typing.

JAMIE
Sorry.

MATT
Say bulge again.

JAMIE
It's a big bulge.

[MATT SHUDDERS]

A massive bulge.

[HE SHUDDERS AGAIN]

Full of….bulge-eosity.

MATT
[STOPS] Is that a word?

JAMIE
Who cares?! Keep rubbing it!

MATT
Tell you what. I think you should take a shower. Then I can give your groin my full attention.

JAMIE
[LOOKING AT MATT'S CROTCH] Looks like that's not the only thing at full attention.

MATT
[STEPPING OUT OF CHARACTER] Hey. That was pretty good.

JAMIE
[STEPPING OUT OF CHARACTER] Thanks.

MATT
[BACK IN CHARACTER] Now you should hit that shower.

JAMIE
I strip off my shorts again and move to the showers. The water is hot and steamy.

MATT
Tell you what. I think I might take a shower as well. Ah that feels good.

JAMIE
I'm soaping myself up. Getting a really good lather going.

MATT
Where?

JAMIE
In the shower.

MATT
No, I mean, where is the lather?

JAMIE
Oh. It's all over my balls. I turn the water down a little and soap up my balls and start to rub my cock and balls.

MATT
I watch you and I'm lathering up as well.

JAMIE
You sure are. Your huge dangling balls are like grapefruits.

MATT
Grapefruits?

JAMIE
Mandarins. They're like mandarins. Round and hairless.

MATT
I shave them. Like to keep a clean house.

JAMIE
And your big dick is starting to arch straight out and over. It's fucking hot.

MATT
Here, let me get some soap on your back, you hot soccer player, you.

JAMIE
Thanks Coach.

MATT
I stand beside you and rub the bar of soap across your back.

JAMIE
It feels good.

MATT
I drop the soap behind you.

BOTH
Oops.

MATT
I drop down and your arse is right in front of me. I want to stick my tongue inside you...

JAMIE
Do it!

MATT
But I just let my three day growth briefly rub against your arse cheek as I retrieve the soap.

JAMIE
Oh sweet Jesus. I'm shuddering with your breath on my arse.

MATT
I stand up against you but much closer now.

MATT WEDGES IN CLOSE BEHIND JAMIE

JAMIE
I can feel your big fat cock up against my arse. I move my legs apart and you slip your cock between my legs.

MATT
You clench and hold my cock with your thighs.

JAMIE
You've almost reached my bruise.

MATT
I start to rub it back and forth. I want to put some lotion on it alright.

JAMIE
You reach around and grab my cock and start to pull it, still sliding your cock in and out of my legs

MATT
Oh yes.

JAMIE
Does that feel good?

MATT
You bet your arse.

JAMIE
Tell me.

MATT
It feels good.

JAMIE
More.

MATT
It feels *real* good. I start pounding my cock into you. It's hitting your balls.

JAMIE
Oh yeah.

MATT
I'm pulling your big cock harder and faster.

JAMIE
Yes.

MATT
Harder.

JAMIE
Yes. Harder!

MATT
Oh yes!

JAMIE
I want to cum.

MATT
I want you to cum.

JAMIE
I wanna shoot.

MATT
Shoot that load!

JAMIE
I'm gonna shoot!

MATT
Ooh yeah!

AMIE
I'm gonna shoot across the floor!

MATT
I'm gonna cum too. Love the way my cock feels between your legs.

JAMIE
Big cock!

MATT
Yeah.

JAMIE
Big...girthy cock!

MATT
Oh Jesus. Yeah. I'm coming. I can feel it rising from my balls.

JAMIE
Big balls. Shoot coach. Bang my balls with your big cock head!

MATT
I'm shooting between your big thighs!

JAMIE
I feel you shoot against my balls. I wanna cum too.

MATT
Then cum!

JAMIE
I wanna cum!

MATT
Cum, you fucker!

JAMIE
Stick your finger in me.

MATT
What?

JAMIE
Stick your finger in me!!

MATT
Okay! I'm sticking my finger in you.

JAMIE
Right up me!

MATT
Right up you.

JAMIE
Ugh! Yeah! Hit that button! Hit that button, you big-cocked coach! Hit it! Aaagh!!!

THE SOUND OF COLLEGE MARCHING BAND MUSIC AS THEY BOTH COLLAPSE TO THE FLOOR SIMULATING ORGASMS. THE STAGE GOES BLACK FOR A MOMENT. WHEN LIGHTS COME UP THEY ARE AT THEIR RESPECTIVE DESKS, WIPING THEMSELVES DOWN. AFTER A LONG PAUSE...

MATT
Hit that button?

JAMIE
Magic of the moment.

MATT
That was amazing. Almost as good as the real thing.

JAMIE
For me that *was* the real thing. Will you be online next week?

MATT
Same bat time, same bat channel. Goodnight Butt boy.

JAMIE
Goodnight Tigger.

LIGHTS FADE TO NEIL YOUNG SINGING "COMES A TIME."

BLACKOUT.

LIGHTS CHANGE TO INDICATE PASSAGE OF TIME WITH THE BOYS IN SILHOUETTE.

SCENE TWO

THE MEN ARE AT THEIR DESKS.

MATT
So, okay. We've established you don't do the bar or beats or whatever. Where do you go?

JAMIE
I like to stay home.

MATT
Must be quiet.

JAMIE
It usually is. But I do read a bit.

MATT
And what kind of work do you do?

JAMIE
I study 3 nights a week finishing off an Arts degree. Dragged it out over five years but I finish this year.

MATT
And what else?

JAMIE
And during the day I work in a call centre.

MATT
Sounds…exciting.

JAMIE
By 1pm every day I'm ready to blow my brains out. But by the end of the year things should improve. I'll start looking around for something better. Maybe take another year and do my dip Ed. I thought I might be a teacher.

MATT
Well, that sounds like a career.

JAMIE
Did I mention I hate kids?

MATT
That bodes well.

JAMIE
What do you do for a living?

MATT
I work in a music store.

JAMIE
Oh good. You must listen to heaps of CDs.

MATT
It's not that type of music store. We sell musical instruments.

JAMIE
Oh.

MATT
Are you musical at all?

JAMIE
Not really. I played in the school orchestra for about six months.

MATT
So what did you play?

JAMIE
Triangle. I wasn't exactly overworked. Do you play any instruments?

MATT
Piano.

JAMIE
That's fantastic.

MATT
Sometimes you can lose yourself. It's pretty good but I'm not that good. Need to practice more. So...

JAMIE
So?

MATT
Are we gonna that conversation again?

JAMIE
Sorry.

MATT
Don't be sorry. So, do you want to play?

JAMIE
I guess.

MATT
Well, as long as you're sure.

JAMIE
No, I mean, I'd love to.

MATT
Good. Then you start.

JAMIE
Me?

MATT
Uh-huh. Go to town.

JAMIE
I don't know how to start.

MATT
Well, first you come up with a place and you go from there.

JAMIE
Uh, alright. So…where are we?

MATT
It's your fantasy. You tell me.

JAMIE
Of course. My fantasy. Uh. Okay. It's late at night.

THE STAGE LIGHTS START TO GO DIM.

MATT
Good.

JAMIE
[HE GETS UP] During the first world war. It's the trenches in France. 1915. Battle of the Somme. I read about it at high school. The plucky young private is watching the tough and craggy sergeant opposite. It's 2 in the morning. The fog is slowly rolling over the tops of the trenches.

MATT
Wait!

MATT RUNS OFF STAGE AND GRABS A SMALL SMOKE MACHINE AND FOGS THE STAGE A BIT, WAVING THE FOG AROUND THE STAGE WITH A FOLDER FROM HIS DESK. THE SOUND OF DISTANT GUNFIRE, BOMBS AND A SMALL RADIO PLAYING VINTAGE WAR SONGS

Go on.

JAMIE
Good. It's the night before the big push. The rest of the platoon are sitting down the other end of the trench, huddled together and trying to keep warm. But not

our private. He's always been a loner. Ever since he was a kid helping his parents on their farm.. Times were tough…

MATT
Too much background. Get on with the "now".

JAMIE
What? Oh. Gotcha. Like I said. Young private.

MATT
What's he look like?

JAMIE
Who?

MATT
The private.

JAMIE
Oh. Good looking guy. Olive skin. Dark hair. Well-chiselled face. Clean cut. Lean body. No fat. Helping his dad sow the crops has kept him muscled.

MATT
Big arms?

JAMIE
Huge…but not too much. Looks like he could have been a drummer in a band…

MATT
In the trenches in 1915?

JAMIE
Okay. Not a drummer. Could have been on the wharves?

MATT
Good.

JAMIE
Strong upper body and rippled abs. Legs like a bike rider.

MATT
Stay in the period.

JAMIE
Right. And the sergeant sits across from him, his legs splayed across the trench, his muddy boots just inches from the young private's feet. The sergeant is only a few years older. Maybe 25-26. Solid build. Dark hair, almost Hugh Jackman unshaven good looks. A bit rough but very good looking. Even though it's kinda cold the Sergeant has his shirt slightly open revealing a dark hairy chest...

MATT
I don't like too much hair.

JAMIE
It's *my* fantasy.

MATT
Sure.

JAMIE
...dark hairy chest. Shirt open down to the navel, joins up with the tufts of hair go-ing down to his crotch. He is rubbing his hand across his chest. His hand brushes across the nipple which starts to stand straight up. He eyes the young recruit. The private looks at him for a moment then his eyes dart away. He is almost embarrassed to have seen the sergeant touching his own nipple. The sergeant smiles then takes out a rolled up cigarette and lights it.

THE REST OF THE SCENE IS PLAYED VERY HAMMY CAMERA ACTING STYLE

MATT
[VERY CLIPPED ENGLISH] Smith?

JAMIE
[YOUNG AND WITH A LISP] Yes, sergeant.

MATT
What's the matter? Can't sleep.

JAMIE
Guess not, sergeant.

MATT
Same here. Like to look at the stars. May be the last time I'm gonna see them. You never know. You know, the others are fast asleep. You don't need to call me Sergeant. How old are you?

JAMIE
18 sir.

MATT
I'm only a few years older than you. I tell you what. You can call me Tom and I'll call you Peter. That's your name, isn't it?

JAMIE
Apparently.

MATT
Only when no-one else is around, okay?

JAMIE
Sure thing Sarge. I mean Tom.

MATT
Smoke?

JAMIE
Sure.

HE REACHES ACROSS AS THE SERGEANT HANDS HIM HIS OWN CIGARETTE AND LIGHTS UP ANOTHER ONE. JAMIE STARTS COUGHING.

MATT
You do smoke, don't you?

JAMIE
Not really.

MATT
Okay. Well, if ever there was a time to start it's now.

JAMIE
I guess.

MATT
So tell me Peter. You hoping to get out of this hell hole in one piece?

JAMIE
I sure am, Sarge. I mean, Tom.

MATT
Yeah, sure would be nice to get home to the folks and a nice warm bed.

JAMIE
Sure would.

MATT
Damn this war! You got a girl back home, soldier?

JAMIE
No Tom. I ain't.

MATT
That's a surprise. Good looking lad like you must be beating them off with a stick. You got a big stick to beat 'em off with, Pete? I'll bet you have. I'll bet you've had plenty in your time as well.

JAMIE
I guess, but nothing serious. What about you Tom? You got someone waiting back home for you? Some pretty gal got a candle burning in the window?

MATT
Five or six if the truth be told. Keep 'em keen, not kept. That's my motto.

JAMIE
Boy that must be amazing.

MATT
What's that, kid?

JAMIE
All those…girls.

MATT
It's okay. To tell the truth I ain't that much attached to any of them. Sure they're pretty but ain't none of them got anything that comes close to a friendship between two mates. Hang on a moment will ya?

HE GETS UP AND GIVES THE FOG MACHNE ANOTHER BURST.

Much better. Yeah, that's right. No girl ever came close to feeling as good as sharing a cigarette with a mate. You ever been with a girl, Pete?

JAMIE
I've been with plenty.

MATT
I mean *really* been with girl?

JAMIE
Oh, um…

MATT
That's okay kid. I understand. I used to know what it was like to be a virgin.

JAMIE
I ain't no virgin.

MATT
It's nothing to be ashamed of, Peter. It's all part of this crazy messed up two-up game we call life. Tell you what. If we get out of this hell hole you and me could go to one of those whorehouses down in Morocco. I hear you can get anything you want down there. The place is pretty wild. The girls down there are supposed to be spectacular. Anything goes. That's what they tell me.

JAMIE
Sounds great.

MATT
And uh…if girls ain't your style, well, they got plenty of other diversions as well.

JAMIE
I like girls!

MATT
I'm sure you do. I like girls as well. *[GRIMACES]* I was just saying.

JAMIE
[LONG PAUSE] Diversions?

MATT
Sure. Anything you want. *[STANDING UP]* I'm a liver of life, Pete. Why limit yourself to one dish when the world is a smorgasbord? Go crazy at the banquet. That's another one of my mottos.

JAMIE
You really think we could get down to Morocco?

MATT
Why not? It's 1916.

JAMIE
15.

MATT
1915. This war ain't gonna last much longer. You and me, we'll do some real wild tom-catting.

JAMIE
I can't wait.

MATT
That's if we ever get out of this trench. Damn this war! *[HE LEERS AT JAMIE]* But as least we've both had that…special experience. I mean, if we die at least we've known what it was like to die like men…having done *all the things men do*. Be a terrible shame to die for all this when you've never experienced love.

JAMIE
[STANDING UP AND LOOKING AWAY] I have a confession Tom.

MATT
You do.

JAMIE
I've never experienced…love.

MATT
That's okay. At least you're not a virgin. That would be a terrible shame.

JAMIE
I am a virgin, Tom. I lied. I've never been with a woman.

MATT
I'm sorry Peter. I mean I am *really* sorry.

JAMIE
I've never had sex with anyone!

MATT
You poor kid!

JAMIE
I might be dead tomorrow!

MATT
Peter, calm down. Don't go getting yourself upset.

JAMIE
I don't wanna die a *[MOUTHING THE WORD] virgin*! I don't want to die like that!

SHAKING HIM.

MATT
Hey now. Hey now. That's okay. I won't let anything happen to you.

JAMIE
You won't?

MATT
No, of course not. You and me are buddies, right?

HE THUMPS JAMIE'S CHEST.

JAMIE
Ow! I mean...I guess.

MATT
And buddies take care of each other, yeah?

JAMIE
Yeah.

MATT
Then wipe away those tears. I'm gonna take care of you. You won't die a virgin.

JAMIE
[REALLY HAMMY] But how Tom? How? There ain't no women for miles and we can't just order them in.

MATT
I promise you will not die a virgin. Do you trust me?

JAMIE
Of course I do Sarge. I mean, Tom.

HE HOLDS JAMIE'S FACE IN HIS HANDS THEN STARTS RUBBING HIS HANDS THROUGH HIS HAIR AND VIOLENTLY ACROSS HIS NIPPLES

MATT
I promise you that even if we die like dogs in a ditch tomorrow at least you're gonna go out with one great memory.

JAMIE
How are we gonna do that?

MATT
I can think of a few ways for starters.

THEY LOOK DEEPLY INTO EACH OTHERS EYES FOR A MOMENT THEN JAMIE DROPS ONTO HIS BACK WITH HIS LEGS APART AS MATT FALLS AND STARTS POUNDING INTO HIM. MUSIC: 'A LONG WAY TO TIPPERARY' CAN BE HEARD LOUD.

JAMIE
Shove your big fat cock up me, Sarge. That's what I want. Oh yeah.

MATT
Take it you little virgin bitch! Damn this war!

JAMIE GIVES HIM THE THUMBS UP AS THE LIGHTS FADE QUICKLY.

LIGHTS COME UP THEM SITTING AT THEIR DESKS AS IF THEY HAVE JUST ORGASMED. AFTER A LONG PAUSE....

MATT
You know, I think you're getting good at this.

JAMIE
Thanks. That was fun. Though I am starting to wonder how I always get to be on the receiving end.

MATT
Don't worry. We'll mix it up a bit next time.

JAMIE
There's going to be a next time?

MATT
Of course. If you want it, that is.

JAMIE
Yeah. Of course. *[PAUSE]* I was just wondering...

MATT
What?

JAMIE
Well. Maybe we could meet up. You know. In person.

MATT
Oh.

JAMIE
I mean, only if you want to. I don't want to rush you.

MATT
No, it's not that. I'm just thinking, we're having a good time doing this, aren't we?

JAMIE
What? No...of course we are.

MATT
So there's no rush, is there?

JAMIE
I guess not.

MATT
Unless you think there's a need to rush. Unless you're not enjoying it.

JAMIE
What?! No. I love it. You're right. Let's not rush this.

MATT
Okay. So I'll say goodnight?

JAMIE
Yeah, sure.

MATT
And talk to you same time next week?

JAMIE
Of course.

MATT
Goodnight Butt Boy.

JAMIE
Good night Tigger.

BLACKOUT

LIGHTS CHANGE TO INDICATE PASSAGE OF TIME WITH THE BOYS IN SILHOUETTE AGAIN.

SCENE THREE

MATT SITS ON THE GROUND CENTRE STAGE. JAMIE STANDS AT HIS DESK TYPING FOR A MOMENT

JAMIE
It's the English countryside. A few hundred years ago.

MATT
Right.

JAMIE MOVES DOWNSTAGE

JAMIE
The English lord and Master of a grand estate is in the stable standing over one of the stable boys that he has just beaten for some minor transgression. The Master stands majestically over the lad in his britches and white cotton shirt. His well-defined hairy chest...

MATT
Hairy chest again?

JAMIE
That's me.

MATT
Good.

JAMIE
His hairy chest rising and falling with exhaustion. The sweat beads above the tufts of hair exposed below his collar. Sweat runs down his face as well.

MATT
The young stable hand sits on the ground at his feet. His cheap cotton peasant smock is saturated as well. His collar-length, golden blonde locks stick sweat-soaked across his face. He wipes them away to reveal a small tear from his eye. And yet there is a swelling is his britches which he cannot explain. The Master looks at him.

JAMIE
[VERY UPPER CLASS BRITISH] You have been in my service how many years?

MATT
[CORNISH ACCENT] Two, sir.

JAMIE
And yet I have barely spoken to you in that time?

MATT
You have many duties sir. You can't be bothering with a wretched stable hand.

JAMIE
I cannot have spoken more than fifty words to you since you came here.

MATT
No sir. Mr Green. He gives me my orders. You have no need.

JAMIE
It is a shame.

MATT
Shame sir?

JAMIE
Yes. And for that and what I did earlier you must forgive me. I acted harshly.

MATT
No sir. Not at all. T'was your right to take me to task for killing all those sheep.

JAMIE
I do not understand it.

MATT
I don't like sheep.

JAMIE
Well, that's fair enough. Can't abide them myself really. But going at all forty of them with a mallet for a simple dislike seems a tad…overzealous?

MATT
I am truly sorry.

JAMIE
A simple error of judgment. And I…over-reacted. I am sorry. Please say you will forgive me.

MATT
Tis not my part to judge you, good sir. You are a fine and fair man. I see that in your eyes. Kind and giving. Even when you are given cause to whip me I think "what a fine gentleman. He cares about his servants so much that he would use such means to correct their behaviour." A lesser man would not bother and quickly terminate our services. I respect you, sir.

JAMIE
You respect me?

MATT
I surely do, sir. You have been very good to me.

JAMIE
Even when I beat you?

MATT
I don't much mind that, sir. Not from the likes of you. Even as you raise your arm, in my mind I sing your praises.

JAMIE
Really? You like me beating you?

MATT
I've had worse.

JAMIE
Worse than beating?

MATT
[GETTING UP] I don't like to speak ill of previous masters but there was one, sir, who used to brand me when I was wicked or doleful.

JAMIE
Brand you?

MATT
Aye, sir.

JAMIE
You, wicked and doleful? I find that hard to imagine.

MATT
To be completely honest, sir, I did give him cause at times.

JAMIE
Still, he sounds a rogue and a snape. And where did this branding take place?

MATT
In his stables.

JAMIE
I meant, where on your person did he commit this punishment?

MATT
Oh. In a rather delicate place. A part of my body I should not mention for fear of insulting your Christian sensibilities.

JAMIE
I do not shock easily. You must show me.

MATT
Show you sir?

JAMIE
That is correct. I would not have you think of me so easily offended with the more squalid forms of punishment. Come. Show me this mark.

MATT
I meant you no disrespect. Of course I will show you.

HE PULLS DOWN HIS BRITCHES. THE MASTER GASPS AT HIS CROTCH.

JAMIE
I see it!

MATT
What? No, not that. It's here.

HE TURNS AROUND, BENDS OVER AND SHOWS HIS ARSE.

[YELLING BETWEEN HIS LEGS] I think you can still see some scarring.

JAMIE
Yes I see it! But let me look a little closer to investigate the damage that scoundrel has caused you.

MATT
If you like.

JAMIE
*[DROPPING BEHIND HIM AND LOOKING AT HIS ARSE]*How could he deface you like this?

MATT
It's not so bad.

JAMIE
Bah! *[GETTING UP AGAIN]* It is the lowest of villains that would so painfully disfigure the natural beauty of an innocent.

MATT
It wasn't *that* bad.

JAMIE
Let me see once more so that I might ponder this horror. Oh my. *[HE IS ABOUT TO LICK IT]* Such an outrage.

MATT
If you will excuse me Sir. I think it might not be right to be so openly exposed in this predicament for fear your good wife might pass by, as she is want to do many an early summer evening, and to come across such as image as this and myself so publicly compromised and undone.

JAMIE
What?

MATT
Shut the door.

JAMIE
Oh, of course.

HE MIMES CLOSING THE BARN DOOR. WHEN HE TURNS BACK MATT IS DRESSED AGAIN.

There now. *[HE EYES HIM LUSTILY]* Tell me....Hodge, is it?

MATT
Hodge. Yes sir. That is correct.

JAMIE
Tell me Hodge. Do you like sleeping in the stable?

MATT
I do sir. More than any bed. I feel closer to the animals.

JAMIE
Apart from the sheep, of course.

MATT
Apart from them. Evil bastards. Always watching you with their beady little eyes.

JAMIE
I cannot help but think that you would find more comfort in a large bed. The pillows strewn about you willy-nilly. A place to rest your weary head after a long hard day agitating the animals. I have an inkling that you have not lain your body across a mattress filled with goose feather.

MATT
No sir. I have not.

JAMIE
Would you like to?

MATT
And where should I do that?

JAMIE
Why, in my room of course. I have a...big one in there.

MATT
You would let me lie in your bed, sir?

JAMIE
I would have you in my bed, yes.

MATT
Oh sir.

JAMIE
And other places as well.

MATT
Why go all the way up to your room, if you don't mind me saying so, when we could be just as comfy down here?

JAMIE
You dare to deny me this simply request?!

MATT
Would that earn me a thrashing?

JAMIE
Indeed it would.

MATT
Then I must deny you sir!

JAMIE
Ah, so you *do* like a good thrashing, do you?

MATT
Oh yes sir.

JAMIE
I had read a brochure from the continent that spoke of men who are aroused by such conduct. Are you one of those, stable boy?

MATT
I humbly admit that, sir. But please promise you will not reveal this deviance to others. I shall die of shame.

JAMIE
Your secret shame shall not trumpeted about, have no fear. Now where is that whip?

MATT

I am afraid Mr Green has taken it to be cleaned, sir. There was a substantial build-up of crust on it from I-know-not-where and he wanted it cleaned in case you called for it. I can run and get it sir if you feel the need to use it again.

JAMIE

No, no. We can make do.

MATT

And with what did you have in mind?

JAMIE

Why, my hand of course. It is a manly hand, is it not?

MATT

*[DROOLING OVER IT]*My, yes sir. You have a very manly man's hand. Coarse and rough. I am sure it has given much discipline in its time and could give damage if necessary.

JAMIE

Is that what you need Hodge? Discipline?

MATT

Oh yes sir. All you've got would be a nice little diversion for me.

JAMIE

And where should I discipline you?

MATT

How about right across my branded arse? Would that please your lordship?

JAMIE

We shall see.

MATT

And where would you have me?

JAMIE

Right here shall be fine but I think under me would be a good start.

MATT

Very well sir. Like this?

HE GETS DOWN ON ALL FOURS.

JAMIE
Yes, most excellent. And I shall kneel beside you like this.

MATT
Very good sir. Now hit me.

JAMIE
Very well.

JAMIE GIVES HIM A SOLID SMACK TO HIS ARSE. MATT MOANS.

MATT
Oh sir. Thank you for that. May I have another?

HE SMACKS HIM AGAIN.

Ooh, yeah. That's done the trick. Now keep doing it until I tell you to stop,

JAMIE
Very well.

HE STARTS HITTING HIM AGAINST HIS ARSE. MATT CONTINUES TO LET OUT GROANS.

MATT
Right. Now sit on top of me and take me to task for something.

JAMIE *SITS ON MATT'S BACK AND STARTS HITTING HIS ARSE*

JAMIE
How dare you leave this stable in such a condition! I should find that whip and lash you solidly to within an inch of your life!

JAMIE STARTS THRASHING HIM.

MATT
Yes!

JAMIE
And as for all those sheep!

MATT
Those fuckers! Right, now bang me right between the arse cheeks! Give it to me solid, you rich cunt!

JAMIE CLASPS HIS HANDS TOGETHER AND HITS HIM SQUARE BETWEEN THE LEGS. MATT COLLAPSES.

MATT
Thank you sir.

JAMIE
[GETTING UP] Any time, you young scoundrel. Let that be a lesson to you. And now…

MATT
Yes sir?

JAMIE
And now young Hodge I shall let you have your wanton way with me.

MATT
Oh good sir.

JAMIE
Tell me. Is there anything you would like to do to me?

MATT
I should like to mount you from behind, sir. If it's not too much to ask.

JAMIE
Not at all. Like most Englishmen I love being fucked stupid. *[HE BENDS OVER IN FRONT OF JAMIE]* Now climb aboard and give me all your juicy seed, you greatly-hung stable boy!

MATT GETS BEHIND HIM AND SPITS ON HIS HAND.

No, no! Use straw. I like it rough.

MATT
As you wish.

HE STARTS TO POUND INTO HIM

JAMIE
Oh ye Gods that is wonderful! Do me! Do me harder, stable boy! You dirty fucker, do me!

MATT
Ooh so you like a bit of the gutter talk do you? Very well. Take this you pig!

HE SLAMS HARD INTO HIM

JAMIE
Oh yes!!

MATT
You're loving every inch of my massive member.

JAMIE
Oh yes! Roger me rigid. I am a whore! I am *your* whore!

MATT
Make a sound.

JAMIE
I am making a sound.

MATT
No. Not like that. Come on. Make a sound like an animal.

JAMIE
Very well.

HE STARTS HOWLING LIKE A WOLF

MATT
Good. Good. Now, do it like a sheep.

JAMIE
A sheep?

MATT
Yeah. You love it. Come on, my little fluffy one. Be my sheep.

JAMIE
Bah.

MATT
Louder!

JAMIE
Bah. Baaahhhhh!!!

MATT
That's right Barry, Bah, you great fluffy fucker!

JAMIE
Barry?

MATT
That's what I call all my sheep.

JAMIE
Baah! Baah!!

MUSIC STARTS TO BUILD UP

MATT
That's right me lovely. Make all the noise you can as I shove my fat throbbing cock right into your woolly arse. Bleat like a bastard! And after I've shot my load right up your merino minge how about I smash a mallet right across your fat head!!??

JAMIE
Oh, bah, bah, bah!!!

BLACKOUT.

LIGHTS UP ON THEIR DESKS. JAMIE IS FACING THE WRONG WAY. MATT IS HALF ACROSS HIS DESK. AFTER A LONG PAUSE AGAIN.

JAMIE
I noticed I still end up on the receiving end.

MATT
Sorry about that.

JAMIE
Are you going to go to bed now?

MATT
Yeah, I'm pretty knackered.

JAMIE
Oh.

MATT
What?

JAMIE
I don't know. I just thought maybe we could talk some more.

MATT
I thought we'd done enough talking.

JAMIE
But that was sex.

MATT
I am really tired.

JAMIE
Okay.

MATT
Next time?

JAMIE
If you like. *[PAUSE]* I...

MATT
What?

JAMIE
I...really like you.

MATT
Oh. Okay. *[PAUSE]* Goodnight.

JAMIE
[AFTER A LONG PAUSE] Goodnight, Tigger.

BLACKOUT

LIGHTS CHANGE FOR TIME PASSING AGAIN.

SCENE FOUR

MATT
Okay, you be the marine and I'll be the guard.

JAMIE
I know where that's going to end. I don't want to do that. You always take over the fantasy and I end up getting fucked.

MATT
I thought you liked that.

JAMIE
Getting fucked? Not really. Doesn't interest me that much.

MATT
You're only 24. You can't tell me you've made a decision already whether you're a top or a bottom. You need to train those muscles.

JAMIE
All I know is, in all these fantasies I'm copping it one way or another.

MATT
But it's all imaginary anyway. It's not real.

JAMIE
You're too bossy.

MATT
What?

JAMIE
I said you're too bossy.

MATT
I'm not bossy. I just know what I want.

JAMIE
What about what I want?

MATT
Okay, I'm sorry. Then what do you want to do?

JAMIE
I want to be a top.

MATT
Then you have to be more assertive in your role. Although I did meet a dominant bottom once. Pushy little American fucker. It was like an aerobics class without the leotards. "Do me! Do me!". In the end I wanted to do him with an axe just to shut him up. Had an arse like a pack of leeches.

JAMIE
Nice.

MATT
So start.

JAMIE
Alright. So it's the brig of a big American ship late at night somewhere out in the ocean. The sailor is behind bars for disobeying an order.

MATT
What's he wearing?

JAMIE
It's hot with steam all over the place 'cause it's way down in the bottom of the ship so he just has his white sailor's trousers on and black boots.

MATT
I like black boots. We could lick them later.

JAMIE
Shut up. He's very tanned with blonde, tight close-cropped hair and a flat top.
MATT
Sounds really hot.

JAMIE
He is. I mean you are.

MATT
Okay. And you're the guard. All dark looks and emotions and not well liked by anyone. You hate this sailor for keeping you from what you want to do right now.

JAMIE
What's that?

MATT
Jack off in some storeroom over a hot mag you smuggled on board, filled with big-cocked recruits holding their big uncut cocks and shaved balls.

JAMIE
My cock is already getting hard just thinking about that mag. The corridor behind me is dark and I'm almost ready to knock off soon anyway but I keep looking over at you. You're slumped on your bunk against the wall. You're smoking and wiping the sweat running down your hairless chest. You're looking at me real surly like. I watch your hand run down your belly…

MATT
Until it reaches just above my waist band and I look up at you looking at me. You look really hot if a little pissed. You keep sneering at me but I don't care. All I keep thinking about is what it would be like to walk over to the cell bars and peel open the front of your sailor pants, and reach in and pull out that big fat fleshy cock, whose outline I am starting to make out more and more. You look at me looking at your crotch and for the first time in 7 hours that sneer melts into a dirty smile. You turn and stand against the bars of the cell with the bulge from your pants pushing through between the bars.

JAMIE
I imagine you without your clothes on. I imagine us lying on a bed somewhere. On a bed somewhere kissing. I imagine us…

HE STOPS.

MATT
What's the matter?

JAMIE
Do you mind if we stop?

MATT
What?

JAMIE
Stop. I don't want to do this now.

THEY RUSH BACK TO THEIR DESKS. THE SOUND OF RAIN CAN BE HEARD.

MATT
But we're right in the middle of it.

JAMIE
I'm sorry.

MATT
No. Don't be. What did you want to do?

JAMIE
I don't know. Just talk.

MATT
I would've thought talking was the one thing we do far too often. Is everything okay?

JAMIE
Yeah, sure.

MATT
Alright. As long as you're sure.

JAMIE
It's raining outside.

MATT
Yes. I know. It's nice.
JAMIE
I don't like the rain.

MATT
Really?

JAMIE
No. I'm making that up. Of course! I hate it when someone says something and the other person responds with 'really?" "Guess what? My dog died last night." "Really?" " No. I just said that to make conversation!" It's so fucking annoying.

MATT
Oh.

JAMIE
I'm sorry.

MATT
No. That's okay. We're allowed to be pissed off from time to time. Any reason I should know about?

JAMIE
My heart's not in it.

MATT
I don't care about your heart. It's your hot cock I'm thinking about.

JAMIE
I think I'm just tired.

MATT
Nothing on your mind?

JAMIE
No. Not really. Just ignore me.

MATT
If you say so.

JAMIE
It's just…

MATT
Here we go.

JAMIE
It's just...Why don't you ever talk about yourself?

MATT
What?

JAMIE
You never talk about yourself.

MATT
This is coming out of left field. I talk about myself all the time.

JAMIE
That's just play. You don't give anything away.

MATT
I wasn't aware I had to.

JAMIE
Forget it.

MATT
No, no.

JAMIE
It's just...I can't keep doing this.

MATT
What?

JAMIE
Playing these games. Talking like this.

MATT
Isn't this enough for you?

JAMIE
No. I want to hear your voice.

MATT
Why?

JAMIE
Because I need to hear it. I need to know you're real.

MATT
Of course I'm real. Who do you think you've been typing to all these weeks?

JAMIE
But how do I know that?

MATT
How do you know what?

JAMIE
You are what you say you are. You could be a middle aged housewife for all I know.

MATT
And you could've asked me that the first time we talked online. I'm afraid you're going to have to trust me.

JAMIE
Why don't you want to meet me? You were keen at the start.

MATT
I don't know.

JAMIE
You always make excuses. "Later. We'll meet later."

MATT
And we will. Why is it so important all of a sudden?

JAMIE
How long have we been doing this?

MATT
I'm not sure. 2 months?

JAMIE
Then it's hardly all of a sudden, is it?

MATT
I thought we had a good thing happening here.

JAMIE
But it's all just about sex.

MATT
I don't see the problem. Isn't that why we hooked up in the first place? You want to change the rules?

JAMIE
I just want to feel someone's arms around me for a change. I want to go to sleep in someone's arms and wake up with them the next morning.

MATT
In spite of some of the crazy and downright outrageous things we've done I had no idea you were such a romantic.

JAMIE
That's not being a romantic. That's nine parts wishful thinking. To tell you the truth I'm not really as over the top in real life.

MATT
I should hope not.

JAMIE
I really should have been more honest with you at the start.

MATT
You don't have to be too honest with me. I won't disrespect you. I've always thought honesty was a bit overrated anyway. *[PAUSE]* Just out of curiosity…what weren't you being honest about?

JAMIE
About me being…you know…

MATT
Shit. You're not gay? I knew it!

JAMIE
No, no. I am gay.

MATT
Good to hear it. And don't think I didn't noticed how you admitted that a little easier-er now.

JAMIE
No it was about…um…

MATT
Come on. Spit it out.

JAMIE
About being a virgin

MATT
What about it?

JAMIE
I am.

MATT
What?

JAMIE
A virgin. I lied before. I wouldn't know the first thing about having sex. I've never been with anyone.

MATT
But you told me…

JAMIE
I know what I told you.

MATT
And those three other guys?

JAMIE
I just made them up. I didn't want you to think I was a complete washout. Some stupid fucking kid getting his jollies off on his mum's broadband.

MATT
I wouldn't have thought that.

JAMIE
That's easy to say now. Are you disappointed? About me being a virgin?

MATT
No, of course not. But what would've happened if we did meet that first night?

JAMIE
I would have faked it somehow.

MATT
No matter how good you think you are there's no-one I know that can convincingly fake being a virgin.

JAMIE
Or I would've made some lame excuse and gotten out of it.

MATT
Like a broken down car?

JAMIE
Like a broken down car. But then we started talking and we started playing out those fantasies and I got, I don't know, swept away with it all.

MATT
I see.

JAMIE
You're pissed off now, aren't you?

MATT
No. A little surprised. I mean, for a virgin you played out those scenes really well.

JAMIE
Did I?

MATT
Like a pro.

JAMIE
I was always good at composition in high school.

MATT
Bet you had the teachers worried with your stories.

JAMIE
Yes but no-one ever sucked dick in them. As far as I can remember, anyway.

MATT
Good to hear.

JAMIE
Can we meet?

MATT
I…I'm not sure.

JAMIE
Why are you so scared?

MATT
I'm not scared.

JAMIE
Then meet me.

MATT
I just…

JAMIE
What?

MATT
I just don't want to ruin all this. We have a great thing going.

JAMIE
But it's all fantasy.

MATT
It's still better than anything I've had before.

JAMIE
But it's not enough. Not for me, anyway.

MATT
How do you know? You've had nothing to compare it with. You've never been
with anyone.

JAMIE
I want to be with you.

MATT
You're with me now.

JAMIE
It's not the same. I want to feel what your skin is like. I want to kiss you. I want
to smell you. I want to hold you. I want you to hold me.

MATT
You don't know anything about me. You don't even know my real name.

JAMIE
What *is* your real name?

MATT
It's…Matt.

JAMIE
Matt?

MATT
See? Straight away you're disappointed. And that's just with my name. God
knows what you'll think when you actually see my cock.

JAMIE
You mean it's not eight inches?

MATT
I never lie about statistics.

JAMIE
I've seen your cock. I've seen it, sucked it, done everything I could with it.

MATT
Can't be easy being a virgin slut.

JAMIE
You sure don't sound like a Matt.

MATT
And what should a Matt sound like?

JAMIE
I don't know.

MATT
Exactly.

JAMIE
My name's Jamie.

MATT
You're ruining the story again with too much detail. I don't need to know that.

JAMIE
But this isn't a story.

MATT
But it is. What you and I have is just another story. It's just another role we're play-ing. It's just a whole lot less exotic. What we do? All those fantasies? They're endless. We can go anywhere. Do anything. Be whoever we want to be.

JAMIE
But they're not real.

MATT
That's because real life can be such a fucking disappointment! Trust me.

JAMIE
I want us to be together.

MATT
And what happens if we don't hit it off? What happens then?

JAMIE
I don't know. But at least I'll know I tried.

MATT
But you don't know me.

JAMIE
I know all I need to know. I know I love you.

MATT
What?

JAMIE
I said... I love you.

MATT
What are you talking about? How can you say you love me? You've never even met me. You're confusing love with lust. You can't be in love with someone you haven't even laid eyes on and after only a few months. That's just ridiculous.

JAMIE
It's not.

MATT
People are too quick at using that word. Usually it's just some panacea for something that's way more fucked. It's a quick fix to cover the cracks.

JAMIE
Is that really the way you think?

MATT
Of course it is! I don't say these things just to hear the sound of my own voice. You can't be in love with me!

JAMIE
I can if I want to be.

MATT
Okay. You can be. But you're wrong. How can you be in love with someone when you've never even had sex?

JAMIE
They're two different things.

MATT
But how do you know?!

JAMIE
I just do.

MATT
[SARCASTIC] Well, you're so much more experienced than me so I'll just have to take your word for it

JAMIE
You talk all this big talk about having lots of boyfriends. But you never say if you loved them or they loved you. In fact I don't think I've even heard you use that word. Maybe you made all these boyfriends up as well.

MATT
I didn't.

JAMIE
Then I guess I just have to take your word for it as well?

MATT
Yes, you do.

JAMIE
Meet me.

MATT
Not yet.

JAMIE
Then when?

MATT
Why is it that important?

JAMIE
Because I need more.

MATT
And you base this on what?

JAMIE
I don't know. All I know is I want to see you. I want to hold you. I want to smell you. I want you to call me by my *name!*

MATT
We've got a great thing going here. But you want to mess with it. You're asking way too much from me.

JAMIE
How can wanting to be with someone be asking too much?

MATT
It is asking too much if that person doesn't want to be with you!

THERE IS A STUNNED SILENCE

JAMIE
Oh.

MATT
That didn't come out the way I meant.

JAMIE
No. That's okay. I'm sure you know what you meant. You're right. I'm just being stupid. You know better.

MATT
I don't think you're stupid. I feel terrible. I wasn't expecting tonight to go like this. Jamie?

JAMIE
I have to go.

MATT
I'll talk to you next week?

LIGHTS SNAPS OUT ON JAMIE.

Shit.

BLACKOUT.

SCENE FIVE

LIGHTS COME UP ON MATT PACING AROUND THE PLAYING AREA. HE LOOKS AT HIS COMPUTER OCCASSIONALLY. HE PACES SOME MORE THEN SITS AT HIS DESK HOPING FOR A MESSAGE FROM JAMIE. THERE IS NONE. THE LIGHTS FADE

BLACKOUT

SCENE SIX

LIGHTS COME BACK UP ON MATT LOOKING AT HIS COMPUTER. HE GETS UP AND WALKS AWAY FROM HIS DESK. LIGHT COMES UP ON JAMIE. HE SITS WATCHING HIS COMPUTER. MATT LOOKS TOWARDS JAMIE. JAMIE HITS A KEY. MATT'S COMPUTER DINGS. MATT RUSHES BACK TO THE COMPUTER AND SITS AT HIS DESK.

MATT
Hi.

JAMIE
Hi.

MATT
It's been a while.

JAMIE
I guess it has.

PAUSE

MATT
Do you want to talk?

JAMIE
I don't want to play.

MATT
Of course.

JAMIE
I'm sorry I scared you.

MATT
With what?

JAMIE
Telling you I loved you.

MATT
That's alright. I'm sorry I argued with you last time. You have a right to feel the way you want. You may not believe it but I missed you.

JAMIE SAYS NOTHING

Jamie?

JAMIE
I'm here. I have to go.

MATT
Already?

JAMIE
I have to get up early.

MATT
Of course.

JAMIE
If you want…

MATT
Yes?

JAMIE
I'll be at the Flinders Street Station every Friday for the next 3 weeks…

MATT
Flinders Street Station?

JAMIE
Between 6pm and 6.15. I'll wait on the steps. If you want to see me.

MATT
I don't know if I can.

JAMIE
That's alright. Just letting you know.

MATT
Jamie?

JAMIE
Bye.

THE LIGHTS FADE ON JAMIE. MATT LOOKS AT THE COMPUTER THEN SWITCHES IT OFF. THE LIGHTS FADE ON MATT.

BLACKOUT

SCENE SEVEN

LIGHTS COME UP ON JAMIE STANDING IN THE PLAYING AREA, THE SOUND OF A BUSY STATION. MATT IS NOT ON THE STAGE. JAMIE LOOKS AT HIS WATCH. HE LOOKS AROUND. THE LIGHTS FADE.

LIGHTS UP AGAIN. JAMIE HAS CHANGED POSITION. HE LOOKS TOWARDS JAMIE'S DESK. THE LIGHTS FADE AGAIN

SCENE EIGHT

LIGHTS UP. JAMIE STANDS WAITING. HE LOOKS AT HIS WATCH FOR A MOMENT. HE STARTS TO LEAVE WHEN THE MATT ENTERS. THEY LOOK AT EACH, LOOK AWAY. JAMIE STARTS TO WALK AWAY

MATT
Jamie?

JAMIE
Matt? I never thought you'd show.

MATT
Neither did I. I can't stay long.

JAMIE
Oh?

MATT
Yeah. I've got to be somewhere. This is just on the way. To where I have to be, that is.

JAMIE
I see..

MATT
I…just thought I'd stop here on the off chance you were going to be here. Lots of people here.

JAMIE
It's Friday 6pm. A lot of workers going home. Do you want to go and have a drink?

MATT
I can't. Like I said. I've got…

JAMIE
Got to be somewhere. Of course.

MATT
I just wanted to say I'm sorry.

JAMIE
For what?

MATT
For leading you on.

JAMIE
You think that's what you did?

MATT
Didn't I?

JAMIE
No.

MATT
Okay.

JAMIE
It was just a game.

MATT
What?

JAMIE
A game.

MATT
Really?

JAMIE
Of course. What you and me did together, that was all games. Fantasy, like you said. I mean, those things we did? The coach and the soccer player...the war thing...all of it? All just games.

MATT
And about you being a virgin?

JAMIE
Complete rubbish. I've been with plenty of people.

MATT
Okay.

JAMIE
Had you fooled, huh?

MATT
You sure did.

JAMIE
I guess I was better playing it than you thought.

MATT
You really had me fooled. *[PAUSE]* And when you said you loved me?

JAMIE
Love you? How could I love you? Before today we'd never met. We've only known each other down a broadband connection and only then for a few months. That would be stupid. I didn't even know the sound of your voice until now.

MATT
Right.

JAMIE
So you don't have to worry.

MATT
I don't? I mean, I wasn't worried.

JAMIE
I wasn't pining for you or anything.

MATT
Good.

JAMIE
It *was* good.

MATT
It was?

JAMIE
Sure. But that's not who we really are, is it? And all fantasies have to end, don't they? You can't live your lives playing them, can you?

MATT
No, of course.

JAMIE
You have to get real eventually.

MATT
Eventually yes.

JAMIE
So…that's what I wanted to tell you.

MATT
You waited every Friday night for 3 weeks To tell me that?

JAMIE
Well, it was on the way home anyway, but yeah. I thought it would be better to tell you to your face instead of on the net. And I never waited very long.

MATT
What? Oh. Well, I'm glad you cleared that up for me.

JAMIE
Anyway.

MATT
Anyway?

JAMIE
I really have to be going.

MATT
Of course.

JAMIE
It's really been fun.

MATT
It sure has.

JAMIE
Goodbye.

THEY SHAKE HANDS. THEY STOP FOR A MOMENT. MATT LOOKS AT JAMIE'S HAND THAT HE IS STILL HOLDING.

MATT
Maybe I'll see you around?
JAMIE
Maybe.

JAMIE STARTS TO WALK AWAY

MATT
Two people meet!

JAMIE STOPS.

JAMIE
What?

MATT
I said two people meet.

JAMIE
Okay.

MATT
They've never seen each other before. But when they do meet, purely by chance, they get the feeling they vaguely know each other from somewhere. A dream or something. One of them is young, impulsive and probably a little naïve in thinking love will be easy. The other is a fool because when the chance for love comes up, he turns and runs. He's afraid of feeling something real for once in his life. He doesn't let people get too close in case they see there's not much to him except a quick joke and a laugh and they'll think him shallow and boring.

JAMIE
They both sound a little pathetic.

MATT
They are.

JAMIE
What do they look like?

MATT
One is young, thin. A bit regular. Nothing distinguishing about him...but he has a nice smile.

JAMIE
And the other...short, solid, looks like he was a naughty kid but he's very cocky.

MATT
And very sure of himself.

JAMIE
Maybe a little too much. Where do they meet?

MATT
In a railway station. It's late in the afternoon and neither have plans of any importance.

THE LIGHTS START TO FADE TO JUST THEM IN A SMALL LIGHT.

JAMIE
Are they attractive?

MATT
To each other, yes. But they're not striking. I mean, they shouldn't play hard to get. Neither of them are exactly last ham sandwich in Hungry town if you know what I mean. They're just a couple of guys, meeting for the first time by chance. They agree to go for a coffee.

JAMIE
And maybe dinner after?

MATT
Who knows? The night's still young.

AFTER A LONG PAUSE

JAMIE
Are they hung?

MATT
Oh, most definitely!

JAMIE
They sound hot.

MATT
Oh, they are.

BLACKOUT

End